Spring Harvest
Bible Work

One for a purpose:
Unity in Christ

First published in 2017 by Essential Christian
14 Horsted Square, Uckfield TN22 1QG Tel 01825 746530
Email: info@essentialchristian.org   Web: essentialchristian.org
Registered charity number 1126997

British Library Cataloguing in Publication Data

A catalogue record for this book is available from the British Library.

ISBN 978-1-911237-05-1

Designed by Ascent Creative
Printed by Halcyon

Thanks to Denise Anstead, Rt Rev Pete Broadbent,
Steph Osborn & Sue Rinaldi

Contents

About this book

This book is written primarily for groups to use but can also be used by individuals who want to study the subject of unity. The group might be drawn from one church or several churches in an area. You might use the term home groups, Bible study groups, cell groups – we've used the term 'group' as the generic term.

Our hope and prayer is that these seven studies will be part of a journey with lasting implications for the group, the churches represented by those involved, and the communities and networks where God has placed you. We want this to be more than just seven Bible studies. Each study includes practical application to enable you to have a real impact in your family, work-place and community.

It is perhaps helpful to spell out the assumptions that we have made about the groups that will use these studies.

- The emphasis on the studies will be on the application of the Bible. Group members will not just learn facts, but will be encouraged to think, 'How does this apply to me?', 'What change does this require of me?' and 'In what incidents and situations in my life is this relevant?'

- Groups can encourage honesty and make space for questions and doubts. The aim of the studies is not to find the 'right answer', but to help members understand the Bible by working through their questions. The Christian faith throws up paradoxes. Events in people's lives may make particular verses difficult to understand. The groups should be a safe place to express these concerns.

- Groups can give opportunities for deep friendships to develop. Group members will be encouraged to talk about their experiences, feelings, questions, hopes and fears. They will be able to offer one another pastoral support and to be involved in each other's lives.

- There is a difference between being a collection of individuals who happen to meet together every Wednesday (or any day) and being an effective group who bounce ideas off each other, spark inspiration and creativity, pooling their talents and resources to create solutions together: one whose whole is definitely greater than the sum of its parts. The process of working through these studies will encourage healthy group dynamics.

Space is given for you to write answers, comments, questions and thoughts. This book will not tell you what to think, but it will help you discover the truth of God's word through thinking, discussing, praying and listening.

FOR GROUP MEMBERS

You will probably get more out of the study if you spend some time between sessions reading the passage and thinking about the questions. Make a note of anything you don't understand.

Pray that God will help you to understand the passage and show you how to apply it. Pray for other members of the group too, that they will find the study helpful.

Introduction

In a world of brokenness, pain, confusion and lack of trust, surely there are few things more important than the call for the Church to unite? A united body was what Christ longed for before he was arrested because he knew that if the Church could be one and stand together, then more and more people would be drawn to him (John 17). Encouragingly, this cry for Christian unity seems to be getting louder, perhaps because many of the divisions in society are growing wider. In our culture separation, hostility and isolation are seemingly rampant – mentally, physically, tribally, spiritually, geographically and emotionally – and yet the Father calls his children to cross all of these divides by coming together and reflecting his glory. Surely in a world that is torn apart, the reality of a united body becomes even more infectious to those who are lost?

This material is an aid to assist us in thinking about how we can come together, how we can love one another – see each other for who we truly are and work side by side for the sake of the Kingdom. We all know that there is an enemy whose aim it is to tear down and destroy any unity that we may have, and yet the mission of God is victorious over his plans. The devil prowls around trying to wreck relationships, but the Lord draws us together by his Spirit to demonstrate his love to those who don't yet know him. It is time for the Church to rise up in unity - all for one.

The sessions use key Scriptural passages relating to unity and centre primarily on John 17 - Jesus' key prayers to the Father before his death and resurrection. The dream is that more of us would overcome hurdles that stop us from uniting, like those highlighted in 1 Corinthians with Paul, Apollos and the church (session 2). God longs that we would focus on ways that we can work together, not separate into factions. We all have weaknesses and insecurities, but in writing these notes the hope is that we will still be able to discover our place in the body of Christ and serve him together (1 Corinthians 12). John 17 highlights the need for our unity to be tangible so that the world might believe. Seeking unity is not about a church 'bless up' but rather displaying and witnessing the glory found in the Godhead so that others are pointed to Jesus.

Our humanity is a great obstacle to unity, but the hope is that as we look at models for sustaining unity (session 5) from Acts 6 and recognise the role of the Spirit to give us power to walk together from Acts 4 (session 6), we can be better equipped to journey forward as one. Prayer (as modelled by Jesus) is the vital ingredient to aiding us in our unity and therefore these notes conclude with a focus on various prayers that we hope will be a blessing through the months ahead.

May Jesus walk closely with us through these studies, drawing us together as one, that the world may know that we truly are his disciples and he is the Saviour of the world. God bless you on this pursuit with him. Enjoy the adventure!

Gavin & Anne Calver

Session 1: Be United

'Whatever comes out of these gates, we've got a better chance of survival if we work together'
Maximus
(Gladiator movie 2000)

 ## Opening Thoughts

Where in the world do you see examples of clear unity or equally strong examples of disunity? What are some of the contributing factors that lead to this?

 ## Read John 17:1-26

After Jesus said this, he looked toward heaven and prayed:

"Father, the hour has come. Glorify your Son, that your Son may glorify you. For you granted him authority over all people that he might give eternal life to all those you have given him. Now this is eternal life: that they know you, the only true God, and Jesus Christ, whom you have sent. I have brought you glory on earth by finishing the work you gave me to do. And now, Father, glorify me in your presence with the glory I had with you before the world began.

Jesus Prays for His Disciples

"I have revealed you to those whom you gave me out of the world. They were yours; you gave them to me and they have obeyed your word. Now they know that everything you have given me comes from you. For I gave them the words you gave me and they accepted them. They knew with certainty that I came from you, and they believed that you sent me. I pray for them. I am not praying for the world, but for those you have given me, for they are yours. All I have is yours, and all you have is mine. And glory has come to me through them. I will remain in the world no longer, but they are still in the world, and I am coming to you. Holy Father, protect them by the power of your name, the name you gave me, so that they may be one as we are one. While I was with them, I protected them and kept them safe by that name you gave me. None has been lost except the one doomed to destruction so that Scripture would be fulfilled.

"I am coming to you now, but I say these things while I am still in the world, so that they may have the full measure of my joy within them. I have given them your word and the world has hated them, for they are not of the world any more than I am of the world. My prayer is not that you take them out of the world but that you protect them from the evil one. They are not of the world, even as I am not of it. Sanctify them by the truth; your word is truth. As you sent me into the world, I have sent them into the world. For them I sanctify myself, that they too may be truly sanctified.

Jesus Prays for All Believers

"My prayer is not for them alone. I pray also for those who will believe in me through their message, that all of them may be one, Father, just as you are in me and I am in you. May they also be in us so that the world may believe that you have sent me. I have given them the glory that you gave me, that they may be one as we are one— I in them and you in me—so that they may be brought to complete unity. Then the world will know that you sent me and have loved them even as you have loved me. Father, I want those you have given me to be with me where I am, and to see my glory, the glory you have given me because you loved me before the creation of the world. Righteous Father, though the world does not know you, I know you, and they know that you have sent me. I have made you known to them, and will continue to make you known in order that the love you have for me may be in them and that I myself may be in them."

 # Reflection

It's significant to note that after John chapter 17, the title of chapter 18 in the NIV is 'Jesus Arrested.' Judas is just about to lead the soldiers, chief priests and Pharisees to Jesus to bind him and take him off to the High Priest. It won't be long before Jesus will be crucified. As the Son of God turns his thoughts to heaven, he knows that 'the time has come, glorify your Son, that your Son may glorify you' (17:1). In the last moments before we prepare for death we may find ourselves praying for our loved ones, for the world that we are about to leave behind and perhaps for what is to come. Jesus does all of this, but we must also observe that he focuses strongly on UNITY; he longs that the world would know him, and the Church being 'one' is a key ingredient to this happening (17:20-21). Jesus makes a cry to the Father for unity right before he is arrested; it is obviously extremely important for the Church.

This is not a short pithy prayer from Jesus. He pours his heart and soul into it, asking that he might be glorified (17:5) and then turning his attention to his disciples and then to all believers. His longing is that his disciples will be protected from the evil one and that none of them would be 'lost,' that they would be sanctified, but also that they 'would be one as we are one (Father, Son and Holy Spirit) (17:6-19).' As Jesus moves on to pray for all believers we hear him emphasize why he longs for all his followers to be one; 'so that the world might believe that you have sent me' and 'to let the world know that you sent me and have loved them even as you have loved me' (17:21,23).

Jesus prays passionately that the Church may be united. That people from every tribe, tongue and nation would be one because it will point the world to the love and salvation available to them in Christ. Unity is not an option, it is something that is on God's heart for his children, so we can be certain he will aid us in seeking it. In John 17 Jesus prays for unity; a harmony of spirit, mind, heart and will. He's praying that God would do it, not us! We can't force unity. John Stott explains this further, 'our part is not to create this (unity). Patently we cannot. Our responsibility lies in maintaining and expressing it.'[1]

This gift of unity is not a forced conformity, but an expression of the creative diversity within the Godhead. As there is only one 'true God' who manifests himself through the differing functions of Father, Son, and Spirit, so the loving unity of the body of believers is expressed through a rich variety of gifts and ministry. The whole family of God is a beautiful

1   J. Stott, *The Message of John (IVP, 1993)* p248

picture of differing cultures and attitudes, races and gifts, offered to God in worship and ministry that he may be glorified.

We used this passage as a reflection for the beginning of a week-long mission many years ago. Our heart cry was that Jesus would help us to be united as a team – loving one another, releasing and encouraging each other in our gifts and therefore hopefully pointing people towards Christ. Over the week we came into contact with over a hundred young people and as a team we worked together to love and serve them and share our testimonies. On the final night of the mission many of them gave their lives to Jesus. It was so exciting! In the feedback forms afterwards we noted one thing that seemed to be written on the majority of sheets: the reason the week had been a success was because 'the team seemed to really love one another and love us too.' In praying for unity we were actively demonstrating love that answered the cry of the Son of God to point people to himself. It wasn't complicated but we did make a conscious decision to build one another up and not tear down. God is good!

 ## Discussion Starter

What immediately stands out to you in all of this? What do you find most challenging?

 ## Going Deeper

- Do you witness the united church that Jesus longs for?

- What are some of the obstacles preventing this unity?

- How might you personally make a positive contribution to Christian unity?

 **Quote**

'Be united with other Christians. A wall with loose bricks is not good. The bricks must be cemented together'

Corrie Ten Boom

 # What About Me?

Are there two or three things for you personally that need to change or be acted upon as a result of this session?

 # Takeaway

Take a moment to pray and ask the Lord if there's someone with whom you are currently not in unity. If someone comes to mind ask the Lord to show you what to do. Does he want you to forgive them for something that has happened? Maybe you can find a moment to do that in your heart. Perhaps there is something you could do to reach out to them to rebuild or reconnect the relationship. Remember, if you are hurting because of someone else, forgiveness doesn't just let them off the hook; it heals your pain and brings freedom to start over.

 # Prayer

Lord thank you for praying for us as your followers, thank you that you have not abandoned us and that you help us to love one another by the power of your Spirit. Please will you help us to work together and support one another in seeking to be a united Church. Amen.

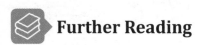 **Further Reading**

You might enjoy reading this book: S. Clifford, *One: Unity – A Personal Journey* (Monarch, 2017).

There is a helpful, brief overview on the Bible and unity here:

http://www.eauk.org/connect/join-us/the-biblical-call-to-unity.cfm

My thoughts and notes....

Session 2: The Struggle For Unity

'Disagreements don't cause disunity,
a lack of forgiveness does'
Loren Cunningham
(Founder, Youth With A Mission)

 ## Opening Thoughts

What are the issues you frequently observe that can lead to disunity? Why do we find unity so hard to maintain?

 ## Read 1 Corinthians 3:1-9

'Brothers and sisters, I could not address you as people who live by the Spirit but as people who are still worldly—mere infants in Christ. I gave you milk, not solid food, for you were not yet ready for it. Indeed, you are still not ready. You are still worldly. For since there is jealousy and quarrelling among you, are you not worldly? Are you not acting like mere humans? For when one says, "I follow Paul," and another, "I follow Apollos," are you not mere human beings?

What, after all, is Apollos? And what is Paul? Only servants, through whom you came to believe — as the Lord has assigned to each his task. I planted the seed, Apollos watered it, but God has been making it grow. So neither the one who plants nor the one who waters is anything, but only God, who makes things grow. The one who plants and the one who waters have one purpose, and they will each be rewarded according to their own labour. For we are co-workers in God's service; you are God's field, God's building.'

 ## Reflection

This is not the beginning of Paul's 'gentle 'brothers and sisters' rebuke; he has already raised his concerns as he begins the letter to the Corinthians. Paul 'appeals in the name of the Lord Jesus Christ, that all of you agree with one another so that there may be no division among you and that you may be perfectly united in mind and thought' (1 Corinthians 1:10). He goes on to reveal that Chloe's household have unearthed the quarrels to him, pointing out that some are following one leader and others, another. Paul must have felt deeply concerned about the factions to raise them again just a short while later. There is a clear issue with some of the church following Apollos, some Paul, others Cephas and others Christ.

The individuals are becoming so highly esteemed that they are being considered on a par with Jesus himself. Paul is quick to say that this is crazy, that none of them are anything without God. Bible teacher Phil Moore puts it this way, Paul 'worked harder than anyone to plant gospel seeds and to water them, but he never forgot that he had no power to save anyone. He shifted the weight of the gospel onto Jesus, where it belongs.'[2]

This quarrelling and jealousy is what is stopping the church from being united and from maturing in their faith. They have got so caught up in who is the 'best' leader to follow, rather than the reality that the Lord is using all of them for different purposes. The people are separating the leaders, whereas the Lord wants to unite them in gifting, vision and perspective. Paul's fight here is to try and deal with all the comparison, jealousy and internal fighting that is taking place and see these challenges replaced with a church seeking to be united instead.

The fact that Paul talks about Apollos and himself in relation to planting shows his emphasis on everyone playing their part. He doesn't separate their roles but highlights how they work together for the Lord to then bless and cause growth. He wants the Corinthian Church to remember that every role is vital and no person or ministry more important than another or effective without each

2   P. Moore, *Straight to the Heart of 1 & 2 Corinthians* (Monarch Books, 2010) p45

other. We are all merely 'servants' of the Lord, not to be worshipped or separated from the rest of Christ's followers. God's love says that the least and the lowest are as valuable as any leader or preacher and we need to treat them as such. This is so challenging for some of our mind sets!

When we think about what conference we are going to go to, or what church appeals to us, we can often be led to attend somewhere if the worship or leaders are what we 'like.' This is not wrong in itself, as long as it is about us drawing nearer to Jesus and being challenged to serve him in some way. The problem is when we begin to put various leaders, events or programmes on a pedestal believing those people and approaches to be the only way, whilst finding fault with other individuals or methods because they aren't what we like.

It's really important for the sake of unity that we can appreciate different ways of doing things. In the last couple of years since Gavin started working for the Evangelical Alliance, he has been privileged to find himself speaking in many different cultural contexts within the UK Church. This has been a real pleasure and a great delight, seeing the Lord on the move powerfully across so many human divides. The wonderful thing is that we remain one body in Christ even though we sometimes do things differently. In heaven, there will not be separate sections for different ages, races, genders or anything else. We will all be united in worshipping for eternity. We need to do all we can to embrace being part of a dynamic and diverse body of Christ in the UK today and accept that others may do things differently but that doesn't make it wrong!

We all have preferences, but style must not be what separates us. Many different expressions of the church have a significant part to play for the Kingdom, and we are in it together – all bringing unique gifts that God in his grace chooses to anoint and use for his glory. Let's keep our focus on Jesus at work through his children by his grace, not our stylistic differences.

Discussion Starter

What immediately stands out to you in all of this? What do you find most challenging?

Going Deeper

- Do you think that Paul's rebuke to the church in Corinth is relevant to the Church today? If so, how?

- Who do you follow? In what ways?

- Does who you follow impact your relationship with Jesus?

- How can we help one another to move on from milk to solid food?

Quote

'Among the unsaved people on earth, what is the prevailing image of Christians today? It's not the dedicated and inspired work of our missionaries. It's not the great preaching of Billy Graham or others who inspire people. It's the image of divisions among brothers and sisters in Christ as we struggle for authority or argue about the interpretation of individual verses in the Holy Scriptures'

Jimmy Carter
(39th President of the United States)

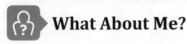 **What About Me?**

Are there two or three things for you personally that need to change or be acted upon as a result of this session?

 Takeaway

Paul recognised that he planted the seed, Apollos watered it and God made it grow. By understanding the role he had to play and the call on his life, Paul was able to find where he fitted in the body of Christ. Finding where you fit helps to remove comparison and jealousy, as well as the potential for quarrels. Do you know what your role is? How the Holy Spirit has anointed you? Why not spend some time this week asking God to clarify where he is calling you to serve. He loves you and has a role for every one of us.

 Prayer

Father forgive us for the times we quarrel with one another or feel jealous towards others. Please will you help us to come against the things that seek to divide us and have a healthy perspective of those who lead and serve. Lord we want you to be our focus and our unity to flow from that. Amen.

 Further Reading

This is a great book on disagreeing in a Godly manner: A. Atherstone, A. Goddard, *Good Disagreement* (Lion Hudson, 2015)

Session 3: The Need For Togetherness

'I can do things you cannot, you can do things I cannot;
together we can do great things'
Mother Teresa

 Opening Thoughts

What do you most admire in those around you? What is it about them you so appreciate and what do you see them bringing that you don't have?

 Read 1 Corinthians 12:12-26

'Just as a body, though one, has many parts, but all its many parts form one body, so it is with Christ. For we were all baptized by one Spirit so as to form one body—whether Jews or Gentiles, slave or free—and we were all given the one Spirit to drink. Even so the body is not made up of one part but of many.

Now if the foot should say, "Because I am not a hand, I do not belong to the body," it would not for that reason stop being part of the body. And if the ear should say, "Because I am not an eye, I do not belong to the body," it would not for that reason stop being part of the body. If the whole body were an eye, where would the sense of hearing be? If the whole body were an ear, where would the sense of smell be? But in fact God has placed the parts in the body, every one of them, just as he wanted them to be. If they were all one part, where would the body be? As it is, there are many parts, but one body.

The eye cannot say to the hand, "I don't need you!" And the head cannot say to the feet, "I don't need you!" On the contrary, those parts of the body that seem to be weaker are indispensable, and the parts that we think are less honourable we treat with special honour. And the parts that are unpresentable are treated with special modesty, while our presentable parts need no special treatment. But God has put the body together, giving greater honour to the parts that lacked it, so that there should be no division in the body, but that its parts should have equal concern for each other. If one part suffers, every part suffers with it; if one part is honoured, every part rejoices with it.'

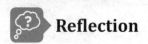 **Reflection**

If ever we needed affirmation that these verses from 1 Corinthians are true and that the Lord really does give greater honour to the parts of the body that lack honour, just check out this well documented list[3] of people he chose to use:

1. Noah was a drunk
2. Abraham was too old
3. Isaac was a daydreamer
4. Jacob was a liar
5. Leah was ugly
6. Joseph was abused
7. Moses had a stuttering problem
8. Gideon was afraid
9. Samson had long hair and was a womanizer
10. Rahab was a prostitute
11. Jeremiah was too young
12. David was an adulterer (not to mention a murderer)
13. Elijah was suicidal
14. Isaiah preached naked
15. Jonah ran from God
16. Naomi was a widow
17. Job went bankrupt
18. John the Baptist ate bugs
19. Andrew lived in the shadow of his big brother
20. Peter denied Christ
21. All the disciples fell asleep while praying (and ran away when Jesus really needed them.)
22. Martha worried about everything

---

3 *Source Unknown*

23. The Samaritan woman was divorced (more than once)

24. Mary Magdalene was demon-possessed

25. Zacchaeus was too small

26. Timothy had an ulcer

27. Paul was a Christian-killer

28. Oh…and Lazarus was dead

We all have flaws (we know we do) but the Bible is full of broken folk the Lord lifted up, called and blessed as they faithfully stepped out to serve him. The Lord is calling a people who will not focus on their own faults or bring down others by commenting on theirs, he is asking us to do the opposite: to build one another up, to honour the parts of the body that lack it and to work together to achieve more for the Kingdom.

Each of us has a responsibility to be real about who we are, accepting that we need one another to achieve what the Lord has ordained for us. If we reflect on David and just think 'oh there was a guy who the Lord deeply loved, who was King and whose family line Jesus came from' without recognising that he was also capable of making a real mess with Bathsheba and Uriah, then we can set one another up for a fall. Our perspective of ourselves and of one another needs to be 'I am a sinner and Christ is a great Saviour' (John Newton). Where we are weak others will be strong enough so that we can carry one another towards glory.

The UK Church has been greatly blessed in recent years by receiving many Christians from all over the world. For many years we sent missionaries to every corner of the world, but today we are receiving them. This is of huge benefit to the Church and brings dynamism and life to a sometimes tired UK Church. Somewhere between 20-25% of UK evangelicals are from a BME (black or minority ethnic) background. This has provided us with a different and hugely exciting landscape.

Not long ago Anne was out for a meal with all the other women from her church. There were 20 something of them there, ranging in age from 16 to over 75. There were at least 10 different nationalities present and it was a very varied group. One of the ladies was asked by a woman on another table what group of people they possibly were. She replied they were from the local church. The woman said 'I thought you were the church. Where else would there be such a diverse group of people altogether.' That sums it up beautifully! The Church is a place for all people, from all backgrounds and corners of the world. That's what makes the body of Christ so rich. This unity in diversity goes against the prevailing narrative of other areas of our culture that are so fractured.

The bride of Christ is at her most beautiful when all cultures, age groups and classes are part of it. We need unity across the divides that other people choose to draw. As Pastor Agu Irukwu, the Senior Pastor of Jesus House in London, and the UK overseer of the Redeemed Christian Church of God (RCCG), said recently to a bunch of white church leaders, 'we're brothers with the same Father but different mothers.' Put another way 'There is neither Jew nor Gentile, neither slave nor free, nor is there male and female, for you are all one in Christ Jesus' (Galatians 3:28). We are one body!

 ## Discussion Starter

What immediately stands out to you in all of this? What do you find most challenging?

 ## Going Deeper

- Do you sometimes feel that 'because you are not a hand, you do not belong to the body?' Which bits of the body seem to be important to the Church?

 Are there people in particular roles that the Church struggles to honour?

 In what ways could we be better at this?

 Which Bible character do you relate to the most from the list on page 20? Do you relate to their flaws as well as the way God gifted and used them? Share together.

 Is there anyone that God is calling you to get alongside to use your gifts together?

 ## Quote

'If you want to go fast, go alone.
If you want to go far, go together'

African Proverb

 ## What About Me?

Are there two or three things for you personally that need to change or be acted upon as a result of this session?

Takeaway

Think for a while about those in your community who are being dishonoured. Who are the people on the fringe of your work place, street, school playground, community centre etc.? What could you do individually or together to show them how important they are to Jesus? Sometimes just a smile can make all the difference! God will be with you as you seek to serve those that are unseen. Recognise them, draw them out and bless them this week in the name of Jesus. If you are struggling, ask the Lord to show you what he would do.

Prayer

Lord Jesus, thank you that we are all part of your body, the Church, and we all have an equally valuable part to play. Please help us to better honour the parts that are unseen and unrecognised for who and what they do. Please enable us not to compare ourselves to others, or think that because we are not gifted in a particular way, that we are not worth bothering with. Jesus, we do not want to be those who shrink back and are destroyed but those who are certain of our identity and confident to step out with you. Amen.

Further Reading

This is a good book on how to use all of your life for Christ and make your own unique contribution to the Body: A. Billington, M. Greene, *The Whole of Life for Christ* (IVP, 2015)

My thoughts and notes....

Session 4: Tangible Unity

'Coming together is a beginning; keeping together
is progress; working together is success'
Henry Ford
(Industrialist, Founder of Ford Motor Company)

 ## Opening Thoughts

What does tangible unity actually look like? What is the best example you can think of where the unity of a group of people has been a key component in the overall success and achievement of the group?

 ## Read John 17:20-23

'My prayer is not for them alone. I pray also for those who will believe in me through their message, that all of them may be one, Father, just as you are in me and I am in you. May they also be in us so that the world may believe that you have sent me. I have given them the glory that you gave me, that they may be one as we are one— I in them and you in me—so that they may be brought to complete unity. Then the world will know that you sent me and have loved them even as you have loved me.'

 ## Reflection

If this prayer from Jesus in John 17 is important enough to utter right before he is arrested, you can guarantee that the devil will be doing all he can to accomplish the opposite. Jesus longs that the unity of the Church would be visible because it will point others to him. The enemy longs to bring a stop to our 'togetherness' – breaking it and loosening it in any way he can to drive people away from the Father. Tangible unity will come under threat from every angle - not creatively, but definitely consistently - and this attack must not stop us from seeking out such clear unity nonetheless.

Let's think for a moment about an example in the world of a unit working together in an amazing way to accomplish a common purpose:

We are both big football fans who reckon we have a good eye for what might be possible, yet like most of our fellow football following friends, we were utterly flummoxed by Leicester City winning the English Premier League in 2016. It's always possible for an unlikely team to win a cup competition, but for such minnows to win the League was utterly incredible. If you put teamwork ahead of personal achievement and plaudits then who knows what might happen?! In a sporting sense, the sky's the limit.

Initially seen as 5000-1 outsiders to win the League, the Leicester players gave every ounce of blood, sweat and tears to the cause and in the end pulled off the most remarkable of victories. Their team of largely unknown players came together to form a formidable unit. The other sides they were competing with were littered with household names supposedly worth tens of millions of pounds, but this Leicester side made up of average players, veterans, and those who'd been rejected elsewhere, went on to be the winners.

Just imagine what might be possible for the Church if we went along a path not entirely dissimilar to that of Leicester City. What might it be like for us to be truly united, giving all that we could to the overarching cause and serving together in a clear, committed and selfless way? This unity of the Church would be compelling to those outside of it. Others would clearly sense it in us and would be intrigued by it, as it would be so counter cultural. Any unity within the Church must be tangible, unmissable to those around us. This may all seem like some unachievable utopian dream, but if a football team can break the rules of what is seemingly possible then the Church is more than capable of doing the same.

If this clear unity could be achieved then it would, in turn, have the incredible potential of helping the world to believe (verse 21) that Jesus was sent by the Father and that the Father loves the Church. "This unity would make a definite impact on the world. Just as Jesus disclosed the unseen God to the world by becoming flesh (1:14), so the Church can be a visible revelation of the unseen Father and his love. The world needs to see our unity in order to see Jesus."[4]

Achieving tangible unity is no easy thing though. Stylistic preferences, cultural challenges and theological differences are just some of the potential obstacles to unity. However, it is still more than possible. Unity is not simply agreeing over the lowest common denominator but is gathering around a shared cause as the people of God. In his role at the Evangelical Alliance, Gavin has found it really challenging, and equally encouraging, to experience serving in a unity ministry first hand. The thousands of churches and individuals, hundreds of organisations and eighty or so denominations that are members of the EA will disagree on some things but find enough to agree on, and a statement of faith to gather around, to make dynamic unity possible.

There are other barriers to unity that we need to be aware of and fight against. A clear issue we often face is the incessant 'friendly fire' within the church. Us Christians need to stop having a go at each other so much and realise that our common goal is reaching the world. It's all too easy to take shots at one another, when in truth we need to do all we can to avoid this. In particular a few of us could learn to be a bit slower to criticize on social media. The whole world is watching the Christians fighting amongst themselves on Twitter!

We need to be a united family and this will often involve being quick to say sorry and fast to forget previous misdemeanours. We remember clearly in our marriage preparation being told to 'never go to bed on an argument.' Further advice was given to say sorry quickly and not worry too much about

---

4   B. Milne, *The Message of John* (IVP, 1993) p248

whose fault it was. Perhaps we should take this principle on as Church. How powerful it would be to be part of a bride that never went to bed on an argument again!

A great way to express unity in a way the world will notice is for different churches to serve together. Social action projects such as Street Pastors, Foodbanks or CAP debt centres provide a wonderful opportunity for Christians to work together and bless their community as one.

This tangible unity needs to be expressed beyond just the Church too. In our friendships, marriages, families and more it's vital that we, as the Church, demonstrate unity to the world that's watching us.

 ## Discussion Starter

What immediately stands out to you in all of this? What do you find most challenging?

 ## Going Deeper

- What are the opportunities within your community for the Church to express tangible unity?

- Where is there too much 'friendly fire' going on? How might this cease?

- Do you need to say sorry to another Christian for what you've thought, said or done to them? Don't go to bed on that argument again.

 ## Quote

'We are only as strong as we are united, as weak as we are divided'

J.K. Rowling
(Author)

What About Me?

Are there two or three things for you personally that need to change or be acted upon as a result of this session?

 ## Takeaway

How can you be a greater part of Christian unity in your community? What can you do to bring peace in your relationships and tangible unity amongst Christians? A lot of this starts by loving the place you live and where you spend your time. Have a go at praying around the area you live in. In truth, most of us will find this easiest as a prayer walk, though we find it better to do this running, so don't feel restricted in the how. Just get out there and ask the Lord for his heart for your community. Then ask him if there are greater ways that the Church can manifest unity within your community and what your role is in this.

 ## Prayer

Lord help us to be more united as your Church. Where this is not the case, bring your healing and let us all be reconciled to one another. We long for the world to see our tangible unity. Jesus, in your mercy, open the eyes of those around us who don't know you to see the unity we are expressing and to be challenged by it. Forgive us for when we are not united and help us to love one another more. Amen.

 ## Further Reading

There's a good selection of simple social action projects to help churches show tangible unity locally at : http://www.cinnamonnetwork.co.uk/projects/

The EA statement of faith: http://www.eauk.org/connect/about-us/basis-of-faith.cfm

Session 5: Sustaining Unity

'The snowflake is one of nature's most fragile things, but just look at what they can do when they stick together'

Vesta Kelly
(Motivational Writer)

 ## Opening Thoughts

Why does the Church so often struggle to maintain a united front? What can we change to begin to make this easier?

 ## Read Acts 6:1-7

'In those days when the number of disciples was increasing, the Hellenistic Jews among them complained against the Hebraic Jews because their widows were being overlooked in the daily distribution of food. So the Twelve gathered all the disciples together and said, "It would not be right for us to neglect the ministry of the word of God in order to wait on tables. Brothers and sisters, choose seven men from among you who are known to be full of the Spirit and wisdom. We will turn this responsibility over to them and will give our attention to prayer and the ministry of the word."

This proposal pleased the whole group. They chose Stephen, a man full of faith and of the Holy Spirit; also Philip, Procorus, Nicanor, Timon, Parmenas, and Nicolas from Antioch, a convert to Judaism. They presented these men to the apostles, who prayed and laid their hands on them.

So the word of God spread. The number of disciples in Jerusalem increased rapidly, and a large number of priests became obedient to the faith.'

 ## Reflection

In Acts 5 the early church was going through an incredibly exciting, and equally challenging time. The apostles were boldly preaching the gospel and had been locked up for doing so. However, an angel of the Lord had let them out of prison and tasked them with going back to preach the good news once more. When the Jewish Council, the Sanhedrin, were deciding what to do with the apostles they sent for them from prison only to discover they were no longer there. They were astonished to see them preaching once more! The Church seemed to be flourishing! It continued to grow numerically, and unfortunately, as is often the case, with growth comes division and conflict.

The church in Jerusalem was basically made up of two groups of Christians: Aramaic speaking Jews (natives of Palestine), and Greek speaking, Grecian Jews who had been scattered all over the world during the centuries before Jesus Christ came. Although these groups were one family, they were an uneasy partnership. There was a tension between these groups centuries before this moment in Acts 6. We need to remember that in the early church they shared their possessions. Here, the daily allocation of food was the point of conflict. In many ways this seems a really trivial matter, but then again that's so often what happens with conflict. Something small becomes big very quickly. In a sense we are reminded that we are not in heaven yet, but in Church.

The first issue they are facing is a clear disagreement over what is best. When the Church is unified and as a result is thriving (as it was in Acts 5), Satan will always be present, doing what he can to cause dissension between believers and to minimise the impact of any ministry taking place. The apostles wisely decided to put the trouble right at once. They called the community together and asked them to select seven men to be responsible for administering the charitable allocation. The seven are traditionally called 'deacons', although the passage doesn't call them this.

The second issue facing the early church was around roles and importance. An immediate reading of Acts 6:2 portrays administrative work as somehow less spiritual and important than the apostles' work. However, Luke's Greek needs to be looked at more carefully. The work of the twelve disciples and the work of the seven appointed are both called *diakonia* which is a Greek noun meaning 'ministry' or 'service.' There is no difference. Neither of these activities is superior to the other because both are Christian ministries, ways of serving God and his people.[5] There is no hint whatsoever that the disciples considered administrative work to be below them or not of the same value as what they were doing. It was entirely a question of calling.

We are all children of God, made in his image, and we need to discover our unique opportunities to serve. Unity comes from realising our roles within the body and acknowledging our equal worth. When God created us he never intended that we'd all be the same. Human beings have an awful lot in common with one another and yet are each profoundly unique. We are all made in the image of God (Genesis 1:27) and yet all created distinct. When God made you he threw the mould away. Not because it was broken but because one of you is enough! If you get close to any human being you realise how amazing and special they are, but you also realise that one of them is what is needed. We don't want clones of people, we want each person being comfortable in their humanity whilst embracing the uniqueness of their individuality.

Hard though it may be, we need to be able to say like the psalmist, 'I praise you because I am fearfully and wonderfully made; your works are wonderful, I know that full well' (Psalm 139:14). It's so easy to resent who we are and what we

5   J. Stott, *The Message of Acts* (IVP, 1990) p122

do, and long to be someone else and think it's so much better for others. But God made you to be yourself. In order to serve him fully we need to embrace who we are and be grateful to God for making us as he did. When he created you he didn't make a mistake. Other people may not help with this all the time. We need to fight against the disease of comparison that helps no-one and does nothing constructive within the Kingdom. We are all unique and yet together we are all stronger. We need to pray that we can find ourselves in a place where we are grateful for that for which we were made, whether that is preaching, administration or something different entirely!

This episode in Acts 6 could have been an utter disaster leading to a church split but it turned out in contrast to be catalytic to church growth. The complaints were heard, the conflict was solved, and the church grew. Unity can be maintained, and must be, and in the long-term the fruit of this will be significant.

 Discussion Starter

What immediately stands out to you in all of this? What do you find most challenging?

 Going Deeper

▶ Do you consider what you do for Jesus to have equal worth to what everyone else does? Remind yourself that your Christian service is *diakonia* as much as the Archbishop of Canterbury's is. Allow the Lord to affirm your service of him.

▶ What skills, gifting and opportunities has the Lord given you? How can you use these for his glory?

▶ Who around you is really gifted in a way you admire? Thank the Lord for them.

 **Quote**

'A dream you dream alone is only a dream.
A dream you dream together is reality'

John Lennon/Yoko Ono

 ## What About Me?

Are there two or three things for you personally
that need to change or be acted upon as a
result of this session?

 ## Takeaway

Bring to mind those folks you admire who are
gifted in a different way to you. Thank the Lord
for them again. Now write down what it is you
love about them and why you are grateful to
God for them. Go ahead and make their day by
sending a note, emailing, texting, tweeting or
whatever works for you, but make sure you tell
them today. You will be honouring God because
he made them, and encouraging your brothers
and sisters no end.

 ## Prayer

Lord, help me to be grateful for who you have made me. Protect me from
comparing myself to others or from wishing I had different gifts. I praise you for I am
fearfully and wonderfully made. Help me to live in the truth of that each day. Amen.

 ## Further Reading

It's really a kids book but it's short and the best one we know for reminding us
how special we are to God and how vital in his service: M. Lucado, *You Are Special*
(Candle Books, 2004).

Session 6: That The World Might Know

'The way you store up treasure in heaven is by investing in getting people there'
Rick Warren
(Pastor, Author)

 ## Opening Thoughts

Do you think the world sees the Church as a united body? When the Church is united what impact does it have on those outside of its community?

 ## Read John 17:20-23

'My prayer is not for them alone. I pray also for those who will believe in me through their message, that all of them may be one, Father, just as you are in me and I am in you. May they also be in us so that the world may believe that you have sent me. I have given them the glory that you gave me, that they may be one as we are one— I in them and you in me—so that they may be brought to complete unity. Then the world will know that you sent me and have loved them even as you have loved me.'

 ## Reflection

We read those words of Jesus again; 'so that the world may believe that you have sent me' (21, 23) – that is why we are united, not for our own sakes but to point people to Jesus. Anyone who sees a united Church will be profoundly impacted by it. This is not just about sitting around in cosy huddles being nice to one another, this unity is part of the Great Commission; to go into the world and make disciples. We go out together, in relationship; we do not go alone. Some of the great moments in Church history have been when the Church have put conflict to one side and chosen to embark on mission together. We all long for people from every tribe, nation and tongue to encounter Christ, so therefore let's unite over reaching them with the gospel. Yes, evangelism can often feel like a fruitless task and one that is so hard to do, but if we are engaged in it together, we embody Christ's oneness and demonstrate a powerful message to a divided world.

There is a need for unity within the walls of the Church as well as the togetherness of going into the world. Those we lead to Christ outside of the building can find that the love and relationship they encountered in us is available within wider church life too. We have over 30 different nationalities in our church and one of the things we do is begin our worship in different languages and styles. We are asking; do all people feel welcomed, loved and accepted in this church? If a Muslim comes to faith, do they really encounter the united family of God? Because they absolutely have to if they are made to leave their own flesh and blood! It is a long journey for the Church to truly be Christ's hands and feet, but with his Spirit little steps forward can cause us to make giant leaps.

When Christ tells us to change and become like children (Matthew 18:3) we don't think this means becoming immature. We believe it means we need to recapture the eagerness and enthusiasm of childhood as we seek to reach others. We have two young children and whatever the previous day may have carried, by the next morning they are enthusiastic and eager once more. They get excited about everything, smile a lot and so often see the best where we might see the worst. This is the kind of childlike attitude we need to adopt in reaching the world too. We need to keep going and continue to rekindle enthusiasm in seeking to share the gospel.

Many of us may struggle in evangelism because we think we have nothing to bring and that we're not very good at it. Encouragingly though, we can take the little that we have to offer and with inadequate resources, do things we would never dream to be possible. The plain and simple reality is that with Jesus on our side anything can happen. It's fundamental that as a Church we start witnessing and living out our faith in every environment we find ourselves in. Just as Jesus took a boy's packed lunch (John 6) and fed thousands of people, he can take our small efforts and use them in incredible ways.

We met a girl recently who was feeling really discouraged. She desperately wanted her four college friends to come to faith and none of them seemed to be making any steps towards Christ or indeed having any interest whatsoever. However, as we probed with questions it became clear that these four had all been really hostile to Christ a year or so earlier and now as a result of this girl, they were no longer hostile (though equally not that interested, yet). We turned to the girl and said: 'You should be delighted as your friends are on a journey and you are positively influencing them for Christ even if the progress may seem slow.'

We need to take ownership for some of the places we find ourselves in, and do all we can to reach out to others in those environments. As Christians, we can hold on to the fact that, in the end, it's the gospel we uniquely offer to society. Others who don't know Christ can do everything else too, but we alone carry a gospel message that's truly unique. Therefore let's do all we can to not ever be a Church on mute and let's see a step change in our evangelism here in the UK.

The challenge of Jesus' prayer is inescapable. He envisages and petitions his Father for a unity among his followers which, grounded in a relationship with the Father through Son and Spirit, is sufficiently visible to promote a positive response to the Church in its mission. He finishes where he begins in John 17, that the world doesn't yet know God, but those people who do, need to share him with the world.

Discussion Starter

What immediately stands out to you in all of this? What do you find most challenging?

Going Deeper

How do you feel about evangelism?

What new opportunities are there in your community for reaching others with the gospel?

 The evangelist J. John argues that churches exist for three 'w's': worship, welfare and witness. He also cheekily adds that there's only one of these that you can't do in heaven! If you were to consider the 'w' balance in your church, is there enough witnessing going on?

 ## Quote

'Every Christian is either a missionary or an imposter'

Charles Spurgeon
(Preacher, Author)

 ## What About Me?

Are there two or three things for you personally that need to change or be acted upon as a result of this session?

Takeaway

The American preacher DL Moody was so desperate to see those he knew meet Jesus that he made a list of everyone he wanted to come to faith and committed to pray for them every day. By the time he got to a list of 100 he decided that was enough to be getting on with. 96 of those on the list came to faith before he died, and remarkably the last 4 became Christians at his funeral.[6]

So often we overestimate the importance of our actions and underestimate the value of our prayers. Who could you begin praying for everyday that they might meet Jesus? Perhaps 3 people might be a good start but if you want

6 http://www.worldprayer.org.uk/world-prayer-centre-news/ item/8081-the-power-of-praying-for-friends-who-don-t-know-jesus

to try 100 then go for it! Why not commit to doing this alongside others too so we can continue a united front and hold one another to account.

 ## Prayer

Lord, please help us to be united. Help this unity to be visible to those around us who don't yet know you. Might it lead them to be interested in you and to come to know you personally. Lord we don't want to be united just for the sake of it we want to be united that the world might call you Lord. Help us make this possible. Amen

 ## Further Reading

For a comprehensive collection of stories, reflections, projects, resources and more on how to reach others with the gospel visit the 'Great Commission' evangelism hub at:

www.greatcommission.co.uk

To see how you can be involved in mission and evangelism you might like to read an earlier book of ours: G. Calver, A. Calver, *Game Changers* (Monarch, 2016)

'Those in whom the Spirit comes to live are God's new Temple. They are, individually and corporately, places where heaven and earth meet'

N.T Wright
(Theologian)

Opening Thoughts

Who brings about unity in our churches, families, work places? Are we open to the power of God, through his Holy Spirit, changing our relationships and aiding us in truly loving one another?

Read Acts 4:32-37

The believers share their possessions

'All the believers were one in heart and mind. No one claimed that any of their possessions was their own, but they shared everything they had. With great power the apostles continued to testify to the resurrection of the Lord Jesus. And God's grace was so powerfully at work in them all that there were no needy persons among them. For from time to time those who owned land or houses sold them, brought the money from the sales and put it at the apostles' feet, and it was distributed to anyone who had need.

Joseph, a Levite from Cyprus, whom the apostles called Barnabas (which means "son of encouragement") sold a field he owned and brought the money and put it at the apostles' feet.'

Reflection

Jesus was clear; 'Do not leave Jerusalem, but wait for the gift my Father promised, which you have heard me speak about' (Acts 1:4b). The work cannot continue without the gift, it is vital for the Great Commission to be worked out. It is impossible for the apostles to be the living embodiment of Christ on earth (the Church) without this gift. A couple of verses later Jesus explains what they are waiting for: 'You will receive power when the Holy Spirit comes on you; and you will be my witnesses in Jerusalem, and in all Judea and Samaria, and to the ends of the earth' (Acts 1:8). The apostles were waiting for the gift of the Holy Spirit to come upon them, and when he came it would transform their ministry in a powerful way.

A bit later we read this passage in Acts 4 where the believers are one in heart and mind and sharing everything they had. We cannot ignore the 'wow factor' here... just read that again: they were 'one in heart and mind' – they were in total agreement and they were loving each other so much that they were freely sharing everything they had. Incredible! Now surely this doesn't just come about because they are working for Jesus? Surely this is a result of the power of the Holy Spirit falling on the disciples in Acts 2 and beginning to minister through them in awesome ways? When the Spirit comes he empowers the followers of Jesus to love one another in ways that are beyond our human understanding.

When we think about being unified, this is not something we strive for or give ourselves headaches over; this is something that can freely flow out of lives filled with the Holy Spirit.

When Jesus prays for all believers, he shares with the Father that he has 'given them the glory that you gave me, that they may be one as we are one (Father, Son and Holy Spirit)' (John 17:22). Jesus has given us the Holy Spirit so that we can be united as the Godhead is united. He did not leave us alone when he ascended to the right hand of the Father, no, he sent his Spirit to lead and guide us into all truth together.

The enemy's plans are to 'steal, kill and destroy'. They are about ruining the unity that demonstrates the power of God. In some of those places that you witness breakdown in relationship, where there is slander, gossip, division and isolation, the devil is prowling around in a successful frame of mind!

So often in church life we can see those people who feel isolated and cut off for many different reasons. Sometimes the church knows nothing of why these people feel isolated and so they feel even more separate from the body. Other times the church are aware and doing everything they can to support those who are alone, but it still may not be enough. The enemy twists minds to cause people to feel ostracised, insignificant, unwelcomed and useless, and yet the Lord says that every single part of his body is part of the Temple of God.

It is time to pray!

Let's take a stand again and put on the full armour of God from Ephesians 6:10-18. Let's be strong in the Lord and in his mighty power, and pray that the power of the Holy Spirit will defeat the lies of the enemy and fall afresh to enable us to pull together and love one another freely. It is time to believe these words from Jesus, that he truly has sent the Spirit, and invite him to enable us to walk out in the power of God together. 'God's grace was so powerfully at work amongst the apostles that no one felt any need' – let's pray for that and step out believing that he can minister through us in the same way today.

 ## Discussion Starter

What immediately stands out to you in all of this? What do you find most challenging?

 ## Going Deeper

▶ Do you feel tired of trying to live in unity?

▶ Have you given up believing it can happen?

 In what ways can you begin to pray for unity in your relationships/church/the wider world?

 Why not invite the Holy Spirit to come and fill you afresh, empowering you to live as one, as an active demonstration to the world around you?

66 Quote

'The wizard of Oz says look inside yourself and find self. God says look inside yourself and find the Holy Spirit. The first will get you to Kansas. The latter will get you to heaven. Take your pick.'

Max Lucado
(Author)

What About Me?

Are there two or three things for you personally that need to change or be acted upon as a result of this session?

Takeaway

Why not decide to pray every morning for the next week, asking Jesus to send his Holy Spirit to fill you with power to love the people close to you and those who you come into contact with during your day. Ask him to make you alert to what he is doing in and through you as the hours pass. Perhaps he will ask you to open your wallet to someone unexpected or give something away that you would love to keep. You may find yourself reaching out to help someone in need who you have never served before, or praying for them on the street. Even better – look for ways you can minister alongside others – to increase the glory that will be seen through your efforts. Go for it!

Prayer

Lord thank you for sending the gift of the Holy Spirit to us, your children. Thank you that we do not have to strive for unity but you equip us with what we need. Father please will you increase the power of your Spirit at work in us and through us so that we can be a living demonstration of your love here on earth, Amen.

Further Reading

These two books are really helpful on living by the power of the Spirit in your everyday life.

M. Pilavachi, A. Croft, *Everyday supernatural* (David C. Cook, 2016).

P. Harcourt, *Growing in Circles* (River Publishing, 2016).

My thoughts and notes....

Prayer Responses

Throughout 2017, evangelical Christians of all backgrounds and traditions will be affirming their commitment to unity for mission at numerous events, festivals and conferences. This movement is inspired by the prayer of Jesus that we've looked at in these Bible studies in John 17:21 when he encourages and challenges us to pursue his desire: *"May they all be one that the world might believe"*.

As part of this there are a few different prayers and declarations below that might be helpful to you as a group to do together or to go through individually.

1) A declaration of our shared life in Christ
(to be said out loud altogether)

As believers in the Lord Jesus Christ, through whose life, death and resurrection we are reconciled to God and to one another, we gladly celebrate our unity, identity and common life in him. We rejoice that we belong to the one Father, are redeemed by the one Lord Jesus, and are indwelt by the one Holy Spirit.

As members of the one family, we are united in our commitment to the Lordship of Christ; the centrality of the atoning sacrifice of Christ on the cross, dying in our place; his resurrection; the divine inspiration and supreme authority of the Old and New Testament scriptures; the importance of conversion; and the calling to gospel witness and active service in the world. We rejoice in the unity of the Spirit in the bonds of peace, a unity which transcends the boundaries of nationality, ethnicity, economic status, gender and denomination.

We give thanks for the many expressions of partnership amongst our churches which have declared that unity across the centuries and throughout the world, and we rejoice in the enrichment that is brought to our corporate life by the many diverse aspects of evangelical worship, work and witness.

We repent of those attitudes and actions which have lessened our active commitment to living together as those who are one in Christ Jesus, or which have injured the body of Christ and tarnished our testimony to God's reconciling grace. Seeking to obey Christ more fully, we commit ourselves afresh to prayerful and active unity. By God's grace and through our shared witness, we pray that a fractured world might see and experience the reality of God's reconciling power in the gospel of our Lord Jesus Christ, for the glory of God and his good purposes.

2) A responsive prayer

(Leader to say the text in normal type with everyone affirming the text in bold by saying the words altogether)

Heavenly Father, we thank you for your grace and mercy shown to us through your Son, the Lord Jesus Christ. We acknowledge your greatness and your power and we offer you the worship of our hearts and the service of our lives.

Lord we bring you our thanks and praise

Forgive us the times when we have allowed our differences to become more important than our common convictions, identity and purpose in you. Help us, with your grace, to see Christ in one another and to encourage one another in your Kingdom cause and purpose.

Lord forgive us and renew us

We ask you to give us a fresh understanding of the gospel, an ever-renewing commitment to your Word and a continuing passion for your world. We ask for courage to be faithful to you in our world and we acknowledge our continuing need of the power of the Holy Spirit in our lives.

Lord empower us to be bold in our witness

We pray for a deepening confidence in your purposes for your Church. Help us to celebrate one another, to stand together and to serve together. Always remind us that we are stronger together.

Lord thank you for my brothers and sisters in the faith

We pray that our communities and worlds might see your grace at work in our lives and in our churches. We pray that we may be given boldness in our witness for you and faithfulness in our service of you. Let your Kingdom come on earth as it is in Heaven.

Lord make us a blessing to our communities

We ask you to pour your Spirit upon your church in a fresh way and to draw many people to your Son, the Lord Jesus Christ. May our unity be strengthened in each of our communities by your grace at work in each of your churches and may our witness together bring glory to your name.

Lord restore and revive your Church

These things we pray in the powerful name of your Son, our Saviour, the Lord Jesus Christ.

Amen

3) A shorter prayer

(to be said out loud altogether)

Almighty God,
The Father of our Lord Jesus Christ,
Our only Saviour, the Prince of Peace:
Grant us the grace to see the dangers of our divisions
Take away our prejudice and all that hinders our fellowship
Deepen us in the unity you have already given us in Jesus
And enable us to live as the one body of Christ
Fulfilling the one hope of our calling.

May we in the power of the Holy Spirit
Boldly proclaim Jesus and his power to save
And serve with joy the one God and Father of us all
May we all be one that the world might believe
Through Jesus Christ our Lord.

Amen

Leader's Guide

TO HELP YOU LEAD

You may have led a house group many times before or this may be your first time. Here is some advice on how to lead these studies.

- As a group leader, you don't have to be an expert or a lecturer. You are there to facilitate the learning of the group members – helping them to discover for themselves the wisdom in God's word. You should not be doing most of the talking or dishing out the answers, whatever the group expects from you!

- You do need to be aware of the group's dynamics, however. People can be quite quick to label themselves and each other in a group situation. One person might be seen as the expert, another the moaner who always has something to complain about. One person may be labelled as quiet and not expected to contribute; another person may always jump in with something to say. Be aware of the different type of individuals in the group, but don't allow the labels to stick. You may need to encourage those who find it hard to get a word in, and quieten down those who always have something to say. Talk to members between sessions to find out how they feel about the group.

- The sessions are planned to try and engage every member in active learning. Of course you cannot force anyone to take part if they don't want to, but it won't be too easy to be a spectator. Activities that ask everyone to think about stuff, discuss it or pray into it are there for a reason. They give everyone space to think and form their opinion, even if not everyone voices it out loud.

- Do adapt the sessions for your group as you feel is appropriate. Some groups may know each other very well and will be prepared to talk at a deep level. New groups may take a bit of time to get to know each other before making themselves vulnerable, but encourage members to share their lives with each other.

- You probably won't be able to tackle all the questions in each session so decide in advance which ones are most appropriate to your group and situation.

- Encourage a number of replies to each question. The study is not about finding a single right answer, but about sharing experiences and thoughts in order to find out how to apply the Bible to people's lives.
  When brainstorming, don't be too quick to evaluate the contributions. Write everything down and then have a look to see which suggestions are worth keeping.

■ Similarly, encourage everyone to ask questions, voice doubts and discuss difficulties. Some parts of the Bible are difficult to understand. Sometimes the Christian faith throws up paradoxes. Painful things happen to us that make it difficult to see what God is doing. A group should be a safe place to express all of this. If discussion doesn't resolve the issue, send everyone away to pray about it between sessions, and ask your minister for advice.

■ Give yourself time in the week to read through the Bible passage and the questions and to adequately prepare yourself ahead of the session. However during the session don't be too quick to come in with the answer – sometimes people need space to think.

■ Delegate as much as you like! The easiest activity to delegate is reading the text, but there are other ways to involve the group members. Giving people responsibility can help them own the session much more.

■ Pray for group members by name, that God would meet with them during the week. Pray for the group session, for a constructive and helpful time. Ask the Lord to equip you as you lead the group.

THE STRUCTURE OF EACH SESSION

Feedback: Find out what people remember from the previous session, or if they have been able to act during the week on what was discussed last time. What difference has it made, if any?

Opening Thoughts: A couple of questions to get everyone thinking about the subject to be studied.

Read: It's important to actually read the passage you are studying during the session. Ask someone to prepare this in advance or go around the group reading a verse or two each. Don't assume everyone will be happy to read out loud.

Reflection: This is the main bulk of the material for the session. It's designed to set the scene, open up the passage further and get the group thinking. You might like to share out the reading of this amongst group members but again, don't assume everyone will be happy to do this.

Discussion Starter: An opportunity for each group member to discuss what immediately stands out to them from the reflection or what they find most challenging.

Going Deeper: Some helpful questions to stimulate further discussion and a deeper reflection on the passage.

What About Me?: A chance for each member of the group to consider if there are two or three things for them personally that need to change or be acted upon as a result of the session.

Takeaway: A practical suggestion or idea that might help each member to think further about it all in the week ahead.

Prayer: A simple written prayer that can be shared together as a group and then used again in between sessions.

Further Reading: A suggestion or two of books or similar that may help in further exploring the subject matter covered.

WHAT YOU NEED

Bibles: the main Bible passage is printed in the book so that all the members can work from the same version. It is useful to have other Bibles available, or to ask everyone to bring their own be it paper or electronic, so that other passages can be referred to.

Paper and pens: for people who need more space than is in the book!

Flip chart: it is helpful to write down people's comments during a brainstorming session so that none of the suggestions are lost. If there is not enough space for a flip chart or if having one makes it feel too much like a business meeting or lecture, then try getting someone to write on a big sheet of paper on the floor or coffee table, and then stick this up on the wall.

Snacks & refreshments: nothing quite helps good conversation as much as quality coffee, tea and cake!

GROUND RULES

How do people know what is expected of them in a group situation? Is it ever discussed, or do we just pick up clues from each other? You may find it helpful to discuss some ground rules for the group at the start of this course, even if your group has been going a long time. This also gives you an opportunity to talk about how you, as the leader, see the group. Ask everyone to think about what they want to get out of the course. How do they want the group to work? What values do they want to be part of the group's experience; honesty, respect, confidentiality? How do they want their contributions to be treated? You could ask everyone to write down three ground rules on slips of paper and put them in a bowl. Pass the bowl around the group. Each person takes out a rule and reads it, and someone collates the list. Discuss the ground rules that have been suggested and come up with a top five. This method enables everyone to contribute fairly anonymously. Alternatively, if your group are all quite vocal, have a straight discussion about it!

ICONS

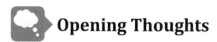 **Opening Thoughts**

 Read

 **Reflection**

 **Discussion Starter**

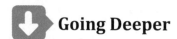 **Going Deeper**

 **Quote**

 **What About Me?**

 **Takeaway**

 **Prayer**

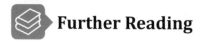 **Further Reading**

THE EVANGELICAL ALLIANCE

evangelical alliance
together making Jesus known

The Evangelical Alliance is the largest and oldest body representing the UK's two million evangelical Christians. For more than 170 years, it has been bringing Christians together and helping them listen to, and be heard by, the government, media and society. Working across 81 denominations, 4,000 churches, 600 organisations and thousands of individual members, it is also a founding member of the World Evangelical Alliance, a global network of more than 600 million evangelical Christians, and partners with Global Connections, the UK evangelical Christian network for world mission.

Unity is the driver — but not just for unity's sake. By bringing people together and following the John 17 mandate to show the immense love of God, they get connected for a shared mission, whether it's nurturing a church culture that is increasingly confident in the gospel, getting involved in community action or lobbying the government for a better society.

The Evangelical Alliance believes the Church is the key to long-lasting change by transforming communities with the good news of Jesus, and in order to inform and inspire Christians in this, provides resources, analysis and articles about society, what the Church is doing and how to get involved. Also, by representing evangelicals to the media, God's truth is presented with grace and good news stories about the difference Christians are making are shared.

For more information visit www.eauk.org

SPRING HARVEST

ec essential christian presents | **SPRING HARVEST**

Spring Harvest is a teaching and worship event for everybody. It's a unique break for all the family: holiday, festival, conference, and an encounter with God. From early morning to late night, Spring Harvest offers a great programme for all the family including interactive all-age worship, prayer and story, excellent Bible teaching, workshops and sessions on a wide variety of topics, celebrations, entertainment and a brilliant youth and children's work.

For more information visit www.springharvest.org

Recommended Resources For Further Study

M Duncan : One for All (Monarch Books, 2017)

500 years after Martin Luther's objections, the Church is threatened with division. With fundamentalists and liberals pulling at either end of the scale, have we forgotten everything that binds us together? Are we focusing too much on the things that could pull us apart? In 2017 Spring Harvest celebrates the theme of unity. Instead of fracturing over secondary issues, we have an opportunity to celebrate a God-given unity centred on mission and the primary truths of faith. We have an opportunity to be One for All.

S Clifford : One: Unity – A Personal Journey (Monarch Books, 2017)

One explores the personal journey of Steve Clifford, General Director of the Evangelical Alliance and looks at the challenges of unity as outworked both in his day-to-day marriage and home life, and national and international relations. Unity is what drives him. The Church is the key to long-lasting change in the world – by working in unity we can transform our communities with the good news of Jesus.

A Atherstone & A Goddard : Good Disagreement (Lion Hudson, 2015)

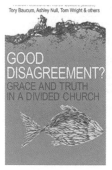

At every level of church life from the local congregation to worldwide denominations, Christians can find themselves in turmoil and divided over a range of important issues. Many conclude that harmony is not achievable, and never will be. Can we, as Archbishop Justin Welby has asked, transform 'bad disagreement' into 'good disagreement'? What would that look like in practice? This book is designed to help readers unpack the idea of 'good disagreement' and apply it to their own church situations.

A Billington & M Greene : The Whole Of Life For Christ (IVP, 2015)

Suppose for a moment that Jesus really is interested in every aspect of your life. Suppose God wants to involve you in what he's doing in the places you spend your time day by day and suppose your whole life is important to Christ... These seven studies will help you live out the marvellous truth that the gospel is an invitation into whole-life discipleship, into a life following and imitating Jesus.

M Lucado : You Are Special (Candle Books, 2004)

Every day the small wooden people called Wemmicks do the same thing: stick either gold stars or grey dots on one another. The most talented and pretty Wemmicks always get the stars, and those who can do little or who have chipped paint, receive ugly grey dots, just like Punchinello. But Eli the woodcarver helps Punchinello understand just how special he is, no matter what all the other Wemmicks may think. In this heart-warming tale, Max Lucado conveys a vital message for children everywhere: that they are special in God's eyes.

G Calver & A Calver : Game Changers (Monarch Books, 2016)

God is the ultimate Game Changer. Through looking at the life of Moses, authors Gavin and Anne Calver address the role and position of the Church in modern society and culture. Broken into five different, thought provoking, sections - Encounter, Engage, Ensemble, Equip, and Empower - Game Changers equips people to step out and change lives and, through the power of God, transform the world around them. Game Changers will challenge and empower churches into being a force for change in the world with the mission of 'Encountering God and Changing the World'.

M Pilavachi & A Croft : Everyday Supernatural (David C Cook, 2016)

The Holy Spirit isn't just for special occasions. It isn't just for hype-drenched Church meetings, or those "chosen" Christians who seem to see miracles at every turn. It's for every person and everyday. And it's definitely not weird. Soul Survivor leaders Mike Pilavachi and Andy Croft dive into the ways God can break into the ordinary. With an abundance of personal stories of living a naturally supernatural life as well as insightful biblical readings and passages, Mike and Andy have made the closest thing to an instruction manual on following God's Spirit as they can.

P Harcourt : Growing In Circles (River Publishing, 2016)

Jesus promised we would grow into fullness of life by His Spirit. Like many things in life, growth is not linear, but happens in seasons and cycles. Neither is there a simple set of steps to follow guaranteeing maturity - that would be too impersonal for a God who loves relationship. Instead, spiritual growth comes from understanding some basic spiritual truths more and more profoundly. This simple, but profound approach to growing in God will reinvigorate your faith and answer many questions about how to develop a vibrant spiritual life.

Other Books From Gavin & Anne Calver

G. Calver : Disappointed with Jesus? (Monarch Books, 2010)

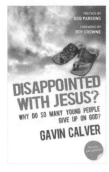

As Gavin Calver had to discover for himself, you can't survive on inherited faith. He found it tough to be the son of a preacher man. Conscious of the eyes and expectations upon him, he got thrown out of Sunday school, slunk off to smoke in the car park during sermons, and eventually abandoned church entirely in favour of Wimbledon football club, girls and booze. Today, still a young man, his passion is to reach the generations that continue to be lost to the faith. This new edition brings his story up to date and spells out his remarkable and ambitious vision of how the missing can be shown the path to personal faith. About 25% of the material is completely new.

C. Calver, G. Calver : On the Front Line (Monarch Books, 2007)

The central theme of this book is what it means to serve Christ with all one's heart. The point is to see how the task has changed, what the challenges are, what really matters and what is secondary. It is easy to fight yesterday's battles! The authors are well able to make this assessment, with Clive's extensive world experience and Gavin's connection with today's generation.

G. Calver, A. Calver : Stumbling Blocks (Monarch Books, 2012)

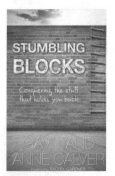

You see a friend suffer. Leaders and churches let you down. Your prayers fall flat. Maybe your dad died. How do you have faith through these things? Gavin and Anne have faced their own challenges. They struggled to conceive – and then their second child needed thirteen blood transfusions. Every day their work brings them into contact with hurting young people. They don't have all the answers, but they demonstrate that it is possible to meet the questions head-on and go on growing.

G. Calver, S. Whiting : Lazy, Anti-Social & Selfish? (Monarch Books, 2009)

There is a widespread myth that young people are feckless and irresponsible. To contradict this, Gavin and Simeon present twelve groups of real young people, and the adults who helped to form, nurture and develop them. Their book explores how these groups began, grew, experienced the presence of God, and acted to change their communities in Jesus' name.

A Calver : Heralding The Coming King' (CWR, August 2016)

Refocus on the true meaning of Christmas with this study for individuals and small groups all about the Gospel account of the nativity. Find out the true biblical account of Elizabeth, Mary, Joseph, Simeon, Anna, Herod, the shepherds, the magi, and of course, Jesus Himself. See how each of their stories connects with Jesus and discover how you too can have a real relationship with the King.

Each of the thirty-one daily Bible studies includes a prayer, questions to ponder and an idea for worship.

A.Calver & A Flannagan : 12 Disciples (Monarch Books, March 2007)

Gritty, unforgettable stories of faith, hope and love that highlight how young people are being good news. Their stories are aligned with teaching on the story of another disciple who experienced similar ups and downs on his journey - Simon Peter. It is a post-modern pilgrims' progress.

OTHER TITLES IN THE SPRING HARVEST BIBLE STUDIES SERIES:

Mission
6 sessions taking inspiration from the early church on how we can be Game Changers in our time.
SHB2137B

Moses
8 sessions to help find your place in God's mission and understand the issues God cares about.
SHB1366B

1 John
Get close to the Source in being, saying and doing.
SHB1839B

Malachi - Wholehearted
Reflections on worship, justice and the faithfulness of God.
SHB1639B

Holy Spirit
6 sessions that look at what it means to live a life empowered by the fullness of the Spirit.
SHB2036B

Romans 8 - Inseparable
Life in Christ, in the Spirit, and in the World.
SHB1351B

Ephesians - United
6 sessions that reflect on the church and living a Christ-inspired lifestyle.
SHB1739B

Daniel – Faith Under Fire
Daniel's faith was literally tested by fire, but his God – and our God – proves himself faithful in the most extreme of situations.
SHB1351B

Passion – Finding An Unshakeable Hope
Exploring the significance of the cross and resurrection for our lives, hopes and relationships will help us grow in confidence and in the character and grace of God.
SHB1319B

Yahweh – God In All His Fullness
7 studies which seek to guide you into a deeper grasp of the magnificence of God.
SHB1389B